Wild Animals

Martyn Bramwell

Illustrated by
Craig Austin

A Piccolo Book

Contents

Introduction   3
Watching Animals   5
Setting Out   7
Animal Sense   8
Natural Clues   10

IDENTIFICATION SECTION
Woods and Forests   12
Hedgerows   22
Mountains and Moors   26
Grassland and Farmland   30
Rivers and Streams   34
On the Coast   38
In the City   41

Naturewatch Projects   44
Nature Clubs   47
Index   48

Editor: Deri Warren
Illustrated by Craig Austin/
The Garden Studio

Designed and produced by
Grisewood & Dempsey Ltd
and exclusively distributed under the
Piccolo imprint by Pan Books Ltd,
18–21 Cavaye Place, London SW10 9PG.
© Grisewood & Dempsey Ltd 1987
ISBN 0 330 29704 X
9 8 7 6 5 4 3 2 1
Phototypeset by Waveney Typesetters, Norwich
Printed and bound in Portugal by Printer Portuguesa.

Introduction

The past 100 years have been very tough for the **mammals** of Britain and Europe. More than 25 countries are crowded into Europe's land area, and these are home to more than 500 million people. Every year, more and more of the countryside disappears beneath our growing towns, cities and motorway networks.

Even more important are the changes caused by farming methods. Over the years lowland marshes have been drained, grasslands have been ploughed up and forests cut down – all to provide more farmland. The traditional picture of the English countryside is a patchwork quilt of small fields separated by hedgerows. For hundreds of years they have provided a safe home for many small animals. But small fields are difficult to farm, and every year hundreds of hedgerows are ripped out to make way for bigger fields that are easier to plough and harvest with large modern machines.

From the air, Europe still looks green and varied. But today the landscape is nearly all man-made. A thousand years ago it was covered with huge forests and rolling grasslands. A few patches of these ancient forests remain, dotted about in remote areas, but most are gone.

Luckily the picture is not all gloomy. Throughout Europe more and more people are becoming involved in **conservation**. **National parks** and other protected areas provide some safety for rare animals, but protecting small local woods and marshes, hedgerows and moors is just as important. And that is something we can all help to do – by taking an interest in our native wild animals and by joining the conservation groups that are helping to protect them (see page 47). That way we can make sure that the badger and dormouse, wildcat and otter are still around to fascinate people many hundreds of years from now.

GLOSSARY

Birds of prey Birds that hunt , such as owls and eagles.

Browsing Feeding by nibbling the leaves of bushes and trees.

Carnivore An animal that eats only (or mainly) meat.

Coniferous Bearing cones. Coniferous forests are forests of pine, fir, larch and other cone-bearing trees.

Conservation Taking action to protect something for the future.

Deciduous Trees like oak, beech and sycamore, which shed their leaves in autumn.

Domesticated Brought under human control.

Estuary The wide part of a river where it meets the sea.

Grazing Feeding by eating ground-level vegetation such as grasses, mosses and lichens.

Habitat The place where a plant or animal lives.

Herbivore An animal that eats only (or mainly) plants.

Hibernate To spend the winter in a kind of deep sleep.

Mammal An animal that gives birth to live young and feeds them on milk.

National Park An area set aside by law for the conservation of the landscape and its plants and animals.

Nocturnal Active at night.

Predator An animal that hunts other animals.

Prehensile Capable of grasping.

Species The scientific name for a particular sort of plant or animal. The tiger, lynx and cheetah are all cats but they are different species.

Track The footprint of an animal.

Trail The pattern of footprints left by an animal.

Watching Animals

Watching wild animals in their natural surroundings is a bit like being a nature detective. To see the animals at all you must first look for the small clues and signs they leave behind in the landscape. These clues include **tracks** and **trails**, the remains of the food they have been eating and the droppings they leave behind.

Mammals are extremely shy and secretive. They have to be like this in order to survive. A few **species**, such as rabbits, squirrels and roe deer, are active during the day, but most are **nocturnal**. Small mammals are constantly in danger from **birds of prey** above and from foxes, stoats and other **predators** on the ground. Keeping quiet and scurrying about in the cover of thick grass or shrubbery during the hours of darkness gives them a much better chance of staying alive.

Clues like these otter tracks may lead you to the animal's regular paths. With patience, skill and a bit of luck, you may then find its feeding and nesting places.

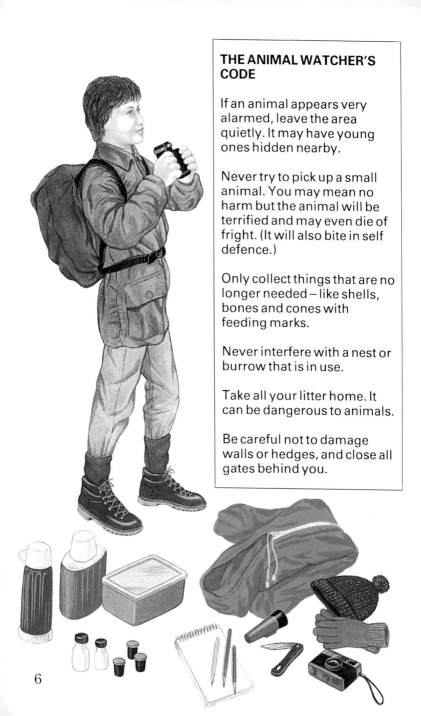

THE ANIMAL WATCHER'S CODE

If an animal appears very alarmed, leave the area quietly. It may have young ones hidden nearby.

Never try to pick up a small animal. You may mean no harm but the animal will be terrified and may even die of fright. (It will also bite in self defence.)

Only collect things that are no longer needed – like shells, bones and cones with feeding marks.

Never interfere with a nest or burrow that is in use.

Take all your litter home. It can be dangerous to animals.

Be careful not to damage walls or hedges, and close all gates behind you.

6

Setting Out

To get the most out of your mammal-watching you need to be safe and warm and comfortable and to have everything you need with you. Remember that animals don't come out and perform just when you want them to. Even when you have found a rabbit warren or a water vole's burrow you may have to sit quietly for quite a long time before the animal comes out into the open.

The golden rules of safety are *never* to go wandering off alone, no matter how well you might know an area, and *always* to take extra care near rivers and streams, in marshy areas and on the coast. The best way is to get one of your parents to join in with you. They will probably have just as much fun as you. Watching wildlife is a great family pastime.

What you wear will depend partly on the time of year and partly on where you are going to spend the day. As a general rule, wear good strong outdoor clothes – walking boots or wellingtons, jeans and a dark-coloured anorak are best. Avoid bright colours, as you want to blend into the landscape as much as possible. If you are in hill country or anywhere likely to be windy or cold, carry a spare sweater in your back-pack along with a woolly hat and gloves. Even a warm summer day can turn cold in the evening, especially in the hills or near the coast. And if you are going to be out all day, take along a packed meal and a flask of soup or hot drink.

The only other things you need are a notebook and pencils for recording what you see (page 11) and some plastic containers in case you want to collect things. Later on you might want to try making plaster casts of animal prints. The method is described on page 46. Two 'extras' which are rather expensive but very useful are a camera and a pair of binoculars. Lightweight 8×30 or 8×40 binoculars are probably the best all-round value.

Animal Sense

Animals in the wild are always on the alert, ready to run away or dive into their burrows at the slightest sign of danger. A shadow falling on the ground nearby could be a hawk swooping to attack. A sudden movement in the grass could be a weasel or fox. So, to get a close view you must always move slowly and gently, keep very quiet, and stay quite still if an animal shows signs of alarm.

Try to imagine the world from the animal's point of view. A human figure looks enormous to a mouse or squirrel. Its shape doesn't 'belong' in the forest. So, if you find a clearing where small animals have been feeding, sit down with your back against a tree or bush. It will help disguise your shape and size. Even if the animals fled at your approach they are quite likely to come out again once the danger appears to have passed.

These squirrels fled when the family first came into view, but the moment of danger is over and the animals have returned to feed on nuts littering the ground.

Noises, too, will frighten animals. Whenever possible let natural sounds cover the noises you make. If you are trying to get closer to an animal, move forward gently each time the wind rustles the leaves or grasses.

Your shape and size are particularly noticeable in open country like farmland and moorland. If you suddenly stick your head and shoulders over a wall or hedge you will scare every animal in sight. Instead, peep through a gap in the hedge, or peer carefully round gateways.

The final tell-tale is scent. Most animals are quite short-sighted. Their warning systems are their ears and noses. You may catch the smell of a fox's den 20 metres away – but the fox will have smelled you coming up to half a kilometre away! In high moorland, red deer may bolt in alarm when you are still two kilometeres away. To stand any chance of getting in close you must always check which way the wind is blowing, and approach the animals with the wind in your face. That way your scent is carried away from the animals, not towards them.

Natural Clues

For safety's sake most animals are very secretive about where they live, especially when they have young ones at home in the nest or burrow. When returning home from feeding or hunting they usually go by a roundabout way, constantly checking that they are not being followed.

Many small animals do most of their feeding not far from home, but larger ones such as foxes, badgers, hares and otters often use regular pathways to and from their feeding and hunting grounds. With practice you can learn to recognize these pathways.

In woodland and along hedgerows, keep your eyes open for acorns, hazel nuts, chestnuts and spruce and fir cones gnawed by small animals such as wood mice, voles and squirrels. Each animal leaves its own special pattern of teeth marks, and by using a field guide to animal signs

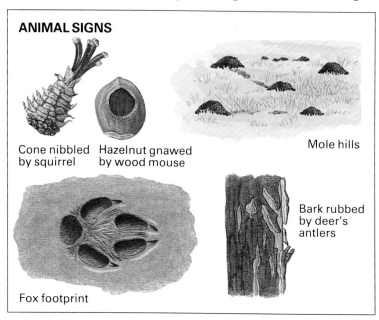

ANIMAL SIGNS

Cone nibbled by squirrel

Hazelnut gnawed by wood mouse

Mole hills

Bark rubbed by deer's antlers

Fox footprint

you will soon be able to identify which animal made the marks. Feeding marks like this can make a fascinating collection.

Whenever you find something interesting – a footprint, an old fox or badger den, a squirrel's drey or a young conifer sapling nibbled by a hare, make notes and sketches in your nature notebook. As the months go by you will build up a large collection of facts about the animals you have seen and about the way they live.

Later you might want to make a neater copy of your notes in a hard-cover nature diary, following your animals' lives throughout the year. Alternatively you could make a wall chart or display from your sketches and the things you have collected.

The most satisfying study of all is to choose a small patch of woodland, a hedgerow or a stretch of stream-bank and try to discover all the animals that live there – who eats what, who lives where, and who hunts who.

NATURE NOTEBOOK

Start each entry on a new page, with a note of the date and exactly where you made the observation. If you are sketching tracks, make a note of the size of the track and how far apart the footprints are. With practice you will be able to tell if the animal was strolling along, running or perhaps chasing another animal.

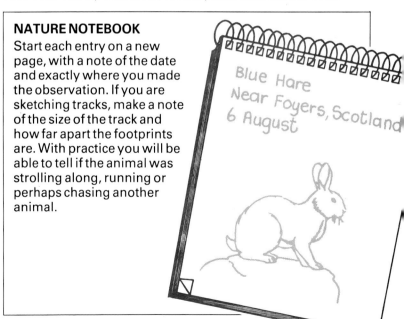

Blue Hare
Near Foyers, Scotland
6 August

Woods and Forests

Woodlands of oak, ash, beech and other **deciduous** trees are often quite rich in wildlife. There is a wide range of food for insects, birds and mammals, and plenty of places to build safe homes. This woodland **habitat** consists of several layers. Fallen leaves and mosses cover the ground. Higher up is a layer of grasses, herbs and wild flowers. Higher still is the shrub layer of bushes, brambles and other climbing plants. And towering over them all is the shady canopy of the trees themselves. Some animals spend all their time in one layer, whilst others, such as the grey squirrel, scamper from layer to layer. This sheltered habitat is the home of the fox and badger, the wild boar, stoat and deer. **Coniferous** forests are less rich in food. They have fewer animals – among them the red squirrel and pine marten.

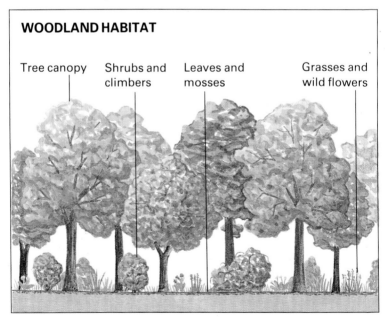

WOODLAND HABITAT

Tree canopy   Shrubs and climbers   Leaves and mosses   Grasses and wild flowers

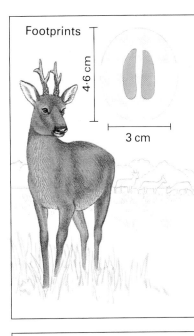

Footprints

4·6 cm

3 cm

ROE DEER

Small, lightly-built deer, reddish-brown in summer but grey-brown in winter. Body pale underneath and white around the tail. Tail itself is tiny, almost invisible. The short upright antlers have three points. Feeds on the leaves of shrubs in woodland where there is plenty of cover. Active by day and by night. Shoulder height: 65–75 cm

DATE_____

PLACE_____

FALLOW DEER

Larger than the roe deer and more varied in colour. Usually reddish-brown with dappled white spots. Winter coat is greyer and the spots are faded. Antlers of the male are very easy to spot. The rear part broadens into a flat blade. Feeds mainly at night on grasses, herbs and berries.
Shoulder height: 85–110 cm

DATE_____

PLACE_____

13

Footprints

6·5 cm

SIKA DEER

A small reddish-brown deer with pale spots in summer. The male has short antlers with few points. Sika deer were brought to Europe from Japan and China and were released in parks. Some now live in the wild. Sika feed in the morning and evening, **browsing** on young shoots of trees and shrubs.

Shoulder height: 80–85 cm

DATE_____

PLACE_____

MUNTJAC

Tiny deer with a red coat. Originally brought from China. Some now live wild in central and southern England and in France. The male has tiny backward-pointing antlers, and small tusks in the upper jaw. Muntjacs feed on grasses, herbs and fruit and also on shrub leaves.

Shoulder height: about 50 cm

DATE_____

PLACE_____

STOAT

The stoat is completely **carnivorous**. It hunts mainly at night, feeding on mice, rabbits, fish, birds and eggs. Found in woodland and in grassland and moorland. Runs fast, climbs well and also swims well. In some areas the coat turns white in winter (except for the black tail tip). Then it is known as 'ermine'.
Body length: 22–30 cm
Tail length: 8–12 cm

Ermine coat

DATE

PLACE

POLECAT

Larger than the stoat, with coarser coat, darker colour, and white face markings. Preys on mice, rabbits and birds, hunting mainly at night. Polecats live mainly in woodland, often close to water, but do not climb or swim as much as stoats. The ferret, used for hunting rabbits, is a **domesticated** form of the polecat.
Body length: 32–45 cm
Tail length: 12–19 cm

DATE

PLACE

15

PINE MARTEN

Sometimes found in mixed woodlands but more typical of coniferous forests of northern Europe. Quick and agile, a superb climber. Often seen in trees where it preys on squirrels, birds and eggs. Also hunts mice and rabbits on the ground. Mainly nocturnal, but is most active around dusk.
Body length: 40–52 cm
Bushy tail: 22–27 cm

DATE_____

PLACE_____

BADGER

The most unmistakable of all woodland animals. Lives in mixed deciduous woods throughout Europe. Badgers are mainly nocturnal but in summer are sometimes active before sunset. They feed on almost anything – worms, small mammals, insects, nuts, fruit and plant bulbs. The burrow, or 'set', has many tunnels and chambers, often with several entrances.
Body length: 65–75 cm

DATE_____

PLACE_____

RED FOX

The fox's main habitat is woodland but it is common in farmland and scrubland as well. The animal is very adaptable and is often found in towns, where it raids dustbins for food. In the wild, foxes hunt rabbits, mice and birds but they also eat eggs, insects and fruit. Foxes are mainly nocturnal.
Body length: 60–70 cm
Tail length: 35–45 cm

DATE_____

PLACE_____

WILD BOAR

Found in deciduous forests across Europe but not in Britain. The boar feeds mainly on acorns, beech mast and bulbs and roots dug up from the forest floor. It is chiefly nocturnal but in summer often spends part of the day resting in the sun. The piglets' stripes help to camouflage them against the forest undergrowth.
Body length: 110–155 cm

DATE_____

PLACE_____

17

Feeding signs

RED SQUIRREL

Europe's original native squirrel lives in all kinds of woodland but prefers coniferous forest. Its main foods are nuts, seeds and young tree shoots. Squirrels are quick, agile and very acrobatic, leaping from branch to branch and often running head-first down tree trunks. They are most active early in the day.
Body length: 19–26 cm
Tail length: 14–24 cm

DATE_____

PLACE_____

GREY SQUIRREL

Grey squirrels were brought to Europe from North America and in many areas they have replaced the native red squirrel – especially in the deciduous forests of Britain. Where the two species meet, they fight – and the grey is bigger and stronger. Both species make an untidy nest or 'drey' of twigs.
Body length: 25–30 cm
Tail length: 20–25 cm

DATE_29/6/05_____

PLACE_Glasgow_____

18

YELLOW-NECKED FIELD MOUSE

Found in all kinds of woodland, orchards and gardens, and sometimes in houses. The field mouse is similar to the wood mouse (page 31) apart from its yellow throat patch. It is very agile, and jumps and climbs well. It feeds mainly on seeds, beech mast, acorns and hazel nuts, and it lives in holes under rocks or amongst tree roots.
Body length: 9–13 cm

DATE_____

PLACE_____

EDIBLE (FAT) DORMOUSE

The largest member of the dormouse family. It is found throughout south and central Europe in deciduous woods and orchards, but only in one small area of England (the Chilterns) where it was introduced about 85 years ago. In summer it makes a mossy nest in a tree hole, but in winter it **hibernates** in a deep burrow.
Body length: 13–19 cm

DATE_____

PLACE_____

WOODLAND BATS

Many people think of bats as rather peculiar and scary animals that live in haunted houses and appear in horror movies. And that is very unfair. It is true that many of them have rather ugly little faces but these tiny creatures are among the most fascinating of all mammals.

For a start they are the *only* mammals that are able to fly, and they do so with amazing skill. Many of them catch their insect food in flight, using what is known as 'echo-location'. The bat squeaks, and the sound bounces off the insect in its path. The bat can then listen for the reflected soundwaves with special parts on its ears and nose.

Many of Europe's bats are now becoming rare. Some are even in danger of disappearing altogether. Old forests are being cut down and old farm buildings are being replaced by modern ones – leaving the bats with nowhere to roost and nowhere to hibernate during the winter months.

Detail of nose

LESSER HORSESHOE BAT

The smallest of the European horseshoe bats, which get their name from the shape of the skin flaps on the face. The bats live in woodland, hunting at night with a fast fluttering flight. They roost by day in holes and caves, sometimes also in the cellars of buildings. Body length: 3·5–4 cm

DATE_____

PLACE_____

NOCTULE BAT

A large, well-built bat with rich golden or reddish-brown fur and long slender wings. It flies high and fast, often 30 metres above the ground and sometimes as high as 100 metres. The flight is straight, with quick turns and sudden dives. Sleeps in tree holes and occasionally in buildings — often in large noisy colonies.
Body length: 7–8 cm

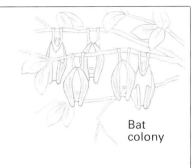

Bat colony

DATE_____

PLACE_____

WHISKERED BAT

Another of the very tiny bats, easily recognised by its unusually dark grey fur and the notched ear. Flies very early in the evening, sometimes even in daylight. Its flight is slow, steady and fluttering. Whiskered bats roost in colonies in summer, but hibernate alone. Never found far from trees.
Body length: 4–5 cm

DATE_____

PLACE_____

21

Hedgerows

Hedgerows provide one of the richest habitats left to the wild animal life of Europe. They offer food, shelter and safety in a landscape almost completely taken over by people and their tractors, crop-sprayers and harvesters. The older the hedgerow is, the more varied the plants it contains – from oak trees, beeches and hawthorns to climbing brambles and wild roses and the carpet of grasses and wild flowers covering the ground below.

Hedges are so thick and tangled that they provide safe roosting and nesting places for dozens of different species. Blackbirds and chaffinches nest there. Moths and butterflies lay their eggs in the foliage and feed on the young leaves. Hedgehogs curl up to sleep in the fallen leaves beneath the hedge, while voles and shrews scurry about in the dense protective cover.

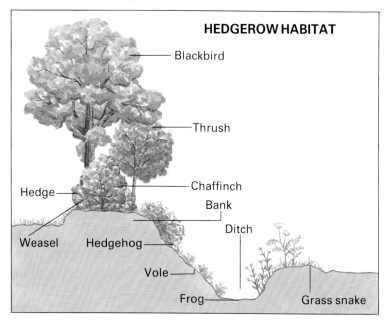

HEDGEROW HABITAT

Blackbird

Thrush

Chaffinch

Hedge

Bank

Ditch

Weasel

Hedgehog

Vole

Frog

Grass snake

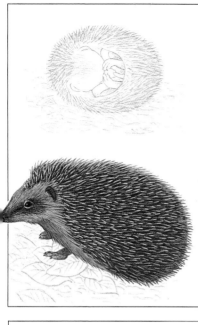

HEDGEHOG
Familiar, spiny-coated animal of hedges and woodland edges. Sometimes found in gardens. Chiefly nocturnal, feeding on slugs, worms, grubs and beetles and also on fallen fruit. Often quite noisy – snorting and grunting as it searches for food. Rolls up into a tight, prickly ball to sleep, or if disturbed.
Length: 20–27 cm

DATE_____

PLACE_____

WEASEL
Smallest of the European carnivores. Distinguished from the stoat by smaller size, short tail without a black tip, and the wavy line separating brown upperside and white underside. The weasel preys on mice, voles, small birds and eggs and is active by day and night. Often stands upright to see over grass and rocks.
Body length: 20–23 cm
Tail length: 6–7 cm

DATE_____

PLACE_____

BANK VOLE
Common in deciduous woods and hedges. Also in conifer forests in Scandinavia. Fur is reddish-brown, often with grey on the flanks. Climbs and swims well. Feeds on seeds, berries and insects. Seen by day more than other voles, but also active at night. Bank voles make complex shallow burrows with many chambers and entrances.
Body length: 8–12 cm
Tail length: 4–7 cm

DATE_____

PLACE_____

COMMON DORMOUSE
Found in hedges, thickets and small woods. Chiefly nocturnal but most active at dawn and dusk. Feeds on nuts, seeds and insects. Summer nest is a loose ball of grass and leaves, usually in a dense bush. Hibernates October–April in a mossy nest in a tree hole or beneath a heap of leaves.
Body length: 6–9 cm
Tail length: 5–8 cm

DATE_____

PLACE_____

PYGMY SHREW

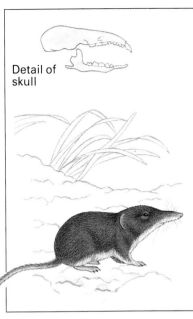

Detail of skull

Tiny insect-eating mammal of hedgerow, grassland and fields. Easily identified by its small size, short back legs, long hairy tail and slender pointed snout. Like the larger common shrew, the pygmy has red-tipped teeth. Active both day and night.
Body length: 4–6·5 cm
Tail length: 3–4·5 cm

DATE_____

PLACE_____

COMMON VOLE

Found in farmland, pastures and hedgerows across most of Europe apart from Spain, Portugal and the Mediterranean coast. In Britain, it is found only in the Orkney Islands. Nests in shallow tunnels, often linked by runways in the grass. Voles are **herbivores**, living on plant shoots and roots.
Body length: 9–12 cm
Tail length: 3–4·5 cm

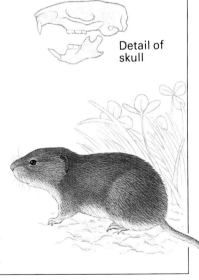

Detail of skull

DATE_____

PLACE_____

Mountains and Moors

The world of the highlands and moorlands is very different from that of lowland fields and woods. Apart from a few patches of high forest there is very little cover. Large animals such as deer, wild sheep and goats are protected from the harsh winds by their thick coats, especially in winter, and must seek shelter in hollows and small valleys if there are no woods nearby.

Many of the smaller animals also have thick fur to keep them warm, and they too seek shelter in the holes beneath piles of rocks, under tangled growths of heather and gorse, and in burrows beneath the ground.

Adult deer, sheep and goats have few enemies in the highlands, but their young – and the smaller hares and voles – are in constant danger from soaring eagles and from nocturnal hunters like the wild cat.

RED DEER
A large, powerfully-built deer. Usually found in dense deciduous forest, but the red deer of the Scottish Highlands have become adapted to life in bleak open moorland. There they stay high in the hills in summer but often come down into the valley bottoms to feed in winter. Mainly nocturnal, feeding on shoots and leaves of trees and moorland vegetation. Shoulder height: 120–150cm

DATE_____

PLACE_____

MOUFLON

The wild sheep, or mouflon, came originally from the islands of Sardinia and Corsica. Now found in many highland regions of Europe, though not in Britain. (A very similar wild sheep is, however, found on Soay Island in the St Kilda group off the Scottish coast.) Easily identified by the rough short coat and large horns.
Shoulder height: 65–75 cm

DATE_____

PLACE_____

CHAMOIS

A goat-like mountain animal with black-and-white face markings, slender horns and a yellow-brown coat which becomes shaggy and almost black in winter. Lives in large flocks in mountain forests and on the bare hill slopes above the tree line. Very agile, active by day, feeding on tree shoots, herbs, lichen and mosses. Not found in Britain.
Shoulder height: 70–80 cm

DATE_____

PLACE_____

BLUE HARE

The blue hare, or mountain hare, is more heavily built than its lowland relative. It has shorter ears and longer legs. In most areas the hare turns white in winter but in Ireland it remains blue-brown all year. Active at night, feeding on grasses and heather, but also often seen in daytime.
Length: 50–60 cm

DATE_____

PLACE_____

WILD CAT

Wild cats are found in dense woodland as well as moorland and rocky hill slopes. In Britain, it is only found in Scotland. It is like a large, powerful tabby cat, with a short bushy tail and striped coat. Most active at dawn and dusk, hunting voles, mice, hares, rabbits and birds. Its lair is a hole amongst rocks, bushes or tree roots.
Body length: 50–80 cm
Tail length: 25–30 cm

DATE_____

PLACE_____

SHORT-TAILED VOLE

Also commonly called the field vole. Colour varies from yellow to dark brown above, with pale underside. Found in fields, woodlands and high, rough moorland. Very common in wet areas. Runs and swims well. The field vole feeds on stems of grasses and reeds and makes shallow burrows and well-hidden runways through the grass.
Body length: 9–13 cm
Tail length: 3–4·5 cm

Winter nest of woven grass

DATE_____

PLACE_____

ALPINE MARMOT

Large, thick-set relative of the squirrel, found mainly in the high grassy pastures of the European Alps between 1000 and 3000 metres high. Often lives in large groups in shallow burrows. 'Sentries' sit upright on their hind legs and give a high-pitched yelp if danger approaches. Marmots feed on grasses and other low plants. Not found in Britain.
Body length: 50–60 cm
Tail length: 13–16 cm

DATE_____

PLACE_____

Grassland and Farmland

In areas of traditional mixed farming, small wild animals can still make a living alongside people. Sheltered places to build burrows and nests can be found in hedges and ditches, in coppices (small patches of woodland with thick undergrowth) and in those corners of overgrown land which the farmer cannot reach with his tractors. Mixed farmland provides a rich choice of food for plant eaters – much to the annoyance of farmers, whose vegetable crops and pastures are often damaged.

Things are much worse for animals in areas of highly mechanized farming. There are few hedges and woods to provide cover, and fields stretching as far as the eye can see are often planted with a single crop, and then sprayed with chemicals. Even the animals that do survive are at risk from the wheels and cutters of harvesters.

RABBIT

Easily distinguished from the hare by its small size, shorter ears and familiar, bobbing run. Lives in grassland, heathland, scrub and open woodland – especially in areas of light sandy soil. Rabbits live in colonies in underground warrens, coming out in the evening to feed on grasses, and on root and cereal crops.
Length: 35–45 cm

DATE_____

PLACE_____

BROWN HARE

The brown (or lowland) hare
has longer ears than the
mountain hare. It lives in
most types of fairly flat
country, especially near
areas of farmland. The hare
is mainly nocturnal, feeding
on grain, crop plants and the
bark of young trees, often
doing a great deal of
damage. It rests in a 'form' –
a shallow hollow scooped
out under cover of rocks or
grass.
Body length: 50–60 cm

Form

DATE_____

PLACE_____

WOOD MOUSE

Despite its name, the wood
mouse is seldom found in
woods. It usually lives in
open country and farmland,
where it lives on seeds,
acorns, hazel nuts and
beech mast. The mice make
burrows with nest chambers
and food stores, but also
make grassy nests above
ground. Mainly nocturnal.
Body length: 7·5–11 cm
Tail length: 7–11 cm

Burrow
entrance

DATE_____

PLACE_____

31

HARVEST MOUSE

Europe's smallest mouse lives in cornfields, long grass pastures and dry reed beds. It feeds mainly on seeds, small fruits and small insects as it climbs among the tall stems using its **prehensile** tail as a fifth 'hand'. The nest is a beautifully woven ball of grass leaves attached to the reeds or hanging in a bush.
Body length: 5–7·5 cm
Tail length: 5–7 cm

DATE_____

PLACE_____

MOLE

The mole spends its whole life burrowing through the soil, leaving tell-tale mounds on the surface of the ground. Its front feet are large and spade-like for digging, and its eyes are tiny – though it is not blind as is sometimes thought. The mole feeds almost entirely on earthworms. Its winter nest is a grass- and moss-lined chamber under a large mole-hill.
Length: 10–14 cm

DATE_____

PLACE_____

COMMON SHREW
The common shrew is an agile insect-hunter found in hedgerows, grasslands, woods, marshy areas and sand dunes. Like the pygmy shrew, it has very sharp, red-tipped teeth. The shrew is active by day and night, moving around in a fast, jerky trot. The ball-shaped grass nest is usually hidden under thick vegetation.
Body length: 6–8 cm
Tail length: 3–6 cm

DATE_____

PLACE_____

WHITE-TOOTHED SHREW
Found on the fringes of woodland, in gardens, dry meadows and grasslands across Western Europe but not in Britain. Like all shrews, it is an insect-eater. Mainly nocturnal but sometimes seen by day. Sometimes enters buildings. Its teeth are all-white.
Body length: 6·5–9·5 cm
Tail length: 3–4·5 cm

Shrew with young

DATE_____

PLACE_____

33

Rivers and Streams

Rivers and streams are especially good places to visit if you want to see a wide variety of wildlife. All living things need water, and so a stream may be just as important to the animals of the surrounding country as it is to the animals that spend their lives in or near it.

In a day by a stream you may see kingfishers, a dipper, a heron or a shy water rail. You might see river trout swimming against the current or leaping from the water to snap up low-flying insects. The shallows and reed beds are full of fascinating creatures – from minnows and sticklebacks to brilliantly coloured dragonflies. Among the river-dwelling mammals are water voles, water shrews and otters. Bats wheel over the water as they hunt for flying insects, while at dawn and dusk deer and foxes may come to the stream to drink.

OTTER
The sleek body of the otter is specialized for fish-catching. It has needle-sharp teeth for grasping its prey, broad feet and a thick powerful tail for swimming. It can also stay underwater for up to six minutes at a time. Otters also hunt on land, taking voles, small rabbits and birds. They nest in riverbank holes, hollow trees and holes beneath tree roots.
Body length: 60–80 cm
Tail length: 35–50 cm

DATE_____

PLACE_____

COYPU

The coypu is a large, plump rodent, originally from the rivers of South America. It was brought to Europe and farmed for its thick fur, but some animals escaped and now live in the wild. In Britain, they are only seen in East Anglia. Coypus live mainly on water plants and are usually left in peace as they do little damage.
Body length: 40–60 cm
Tail length: 30–45 cm

DATE_____

PLACE_____

PYRENEAN DESMAN

This curious relative of the mole lives beside small mountain streams in the Pyrenean mountains of northern Spain. It has large webbed feet and an oar-like tail for swimming. It feeds on small water animals, hunting almost entirely at night, and lives in natural riverbank holes or burrows.
Body length: 11–14 cm
Tail length: 13–15 cm

DATE_____

PLACE_____

DAUBENTON'S BAT

A little bat with quite large feet and a small tail. It lives in woodlands and orchards, always close to water, and usually makes one long hunting flight each night. When hunting it flies low and fast, with rapid wing-beats, swooping low enough to touch the water. It makes a low chirping sound as it flies.
Body length: 4–5 cm

DATE_____

PLACE_____

WATER SHREW

The fur of this large shrew is dark grey, with a silvery underside. The feet are large and fringed with hair. Water shrews are found throughout Europe close to slow-running freshwater streams. They are active by day and night, feeding on insects, frogs and small fishes.
Body length: 7–9·5 cm
Tail length: 5–8 cm

DATE_____

PLACE_____

WATER VOLE

Water voles are the largest European voles. They are found near ponds and streams and also in damp gardens, meadows and marshes. They are skilful divers, even swimming beneath the ice on frozen ponds and streams. The water vole feeds on reeds, grasses and roots, and is most active by day.
Body length: 16–22 cm
Tail length: 10–14 cm

DATE_____

PLACE_____

GROUND VOLE

Ground voles look very like water voles, and can be found in thick undergrowth beside streams, ponds and ditches. However, they are also found far from water in fields and orchards. In Britain, the water vole is found in England and Wales; the ground vole in northern England and in Scotland.
Body length: 12–22 cm
Tail length: 6–10 cm

DATE_____

PLACE_____

On the Coast

Mammals are a very successful group of animals, found in almost every habitat on earth – from the frozen wasteland of the arctic to woodlands, deserts and tropical jungles. Most are land animals but a few groups have learned to live a very different lifestyle.

The bats, as we have seen, have taken to the air. Two other large groups – the seals, walruses and sealions, and the whales, porpoises and dolphins – have adapted to life in the sea. The seals are fast, smooth-bodied hunters, feeding mainly on fish and shellfish and usually spending much of their time in coastal waters. Each year they come out onto land to breed on rocky shores. The whale group, on the other hand, are usually found far out to sea. Only the smaller whales and dolphins are found close to land, and several types may be seen in European waters.

PILOT WHALE

The scientific name of the pilot whale is *Globicephala*. It means 'round head' and describes the high bulging forehead of this type of animal. Pilot whales live in large groups called 'schools' and are seen around the shores of Britain, Scandinavia, France and Holland, and in the Mediterranean Sea.
Length: 4·5–8·5 metres

DATE_____

PLACE_____

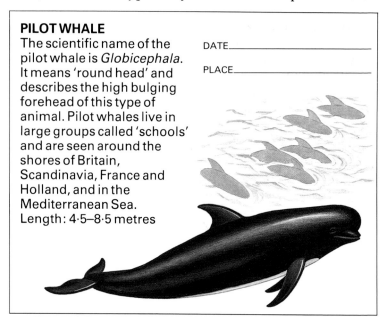

COMMON SEAL

The common seal is grey-white or yellowish in colour, with a dappled coat. It is usually seen on sandy shores and on flat rocky shores – rarely near steep cliffs. It may also be seen in estuaries, feeding on fish and shellfish. Like most seals, the common seal lives in herds.
Length: 1·5–2 metres

DATE_____

PLACE_____

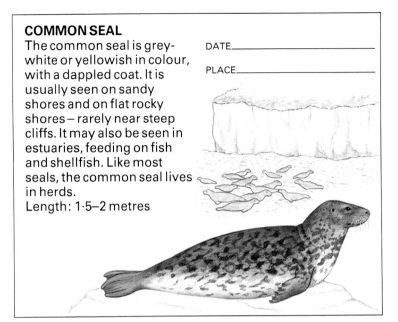

ATLANTIC GREY SEAL

The Atlantic grey is a large seal, weighing up to almost 300 kilograms. The males are larger than the females and have light patches on their dark coats. The females have dark patches on a lighter background. Grey seals are common near rocky shores. They feed on fish and squid and can dive for 20 minutes at a time.
Length (male): 2–3·5 metres

DATE_____

PLACE_____

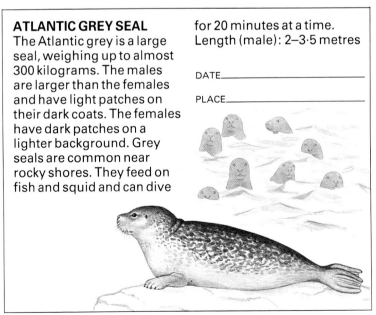

COMMON DOLPHIN

DATE_____

PLACE_____

Dolphins are small, fast, acrobatic members of the whale family. The common dolphin is slender and very graceful, with a long narrow snout or 'beak'. It may be seen all round the coasts of Europe, from Iceland in the north to Spain and all through the Mediterranean. Swims at up to 40 kilometres an hour, often leaping out of the water.
Length: 2–2·5 metres

BOTTLENOSED DOLPHIN

DATE *12· 13· 14· July*

PLACE *Dingle Bay Ireland*

The bottlenosed dolphin is larger and slower than the common dolphin. It is grey-brown to almost black above and pale grey underneath. It has a rather short beak and the lower jaw juts out beyond the upper jaw. The bottlenose is usually found in coastal waters, often in very large schools.
Length: 2·5–4 metres

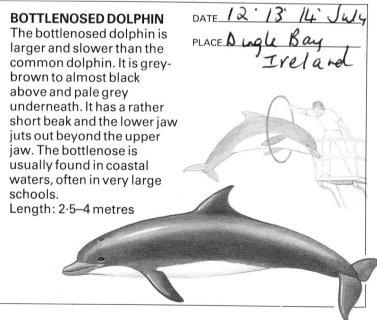

In the City

The gardens and parks of a town or city are very like the natural woodland and hedgerow habitats of many small animals and so it is hardly surprising that we sometimes find them far from the open countryside. Squirrels are common in large parks and gardens. Hedgehogs, field mice and wood mice often come into gardens, and even into buildings, while hares and deer can be a real nuisance in vegetable gardens at the edge of towns.

While these animals are really visitors to the town, others have made the town their true home. Mice and rats are a pest and a health hazard, but they are very successful town dwellers. Bats, too, find roosting places in the eaves and beneath the slates and tiles of houses. Unlike the rats and mice, however, they do no real harm, and deserve to be protected.

HOUSE MOUSE

There are two varieties of house mouse. Those found in buildings are usually dark grey, while those living in fields and gardens are more brownish. Mice are mainly nocturnal. They are very agile, good climbers, and can swim well. They will eat almost anything, but they prefer grain and are a pest wherever food is stored.
Body length: 7·5–10 cm
Tail length: 7–10 cm

DATE_____

PLACE_____

BROWN RAT

The brown rat or common rat probably came to Europe from Asia about 500 years ago. It is a large powerful rodent which swims well and is very common in sewers, on rubbish tips, around farm buildings and along canal banks. In winter, many come into buildings from surrounding farmland. Rats carry diseases and are a major pest in food stores.

Body length: 20–27 cm
Tail length: 17–23 cm

DATE_____

PLACE_____

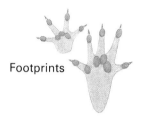

Footprints

BLACK RAT

Smaller and more lightly built than the common rat. It also has larger ears and a longer tail. Black rats climb much more often than common rats and many make their homes in the roofs of barns, stables and warehouses. Also known as the 'ship rat' as it is common in ships and docklands.

Body length: 16–23 cm
Tail length: 18–25 cm

DATE_____

PLACE_____

LONG-EARED BAT

The common long-eared bat is easy to spot, because of its very large ears which meet on top of its head. It has large feet, a fairly long tail and broad wings. The long-eared bat comes out quite late in the evening and often spends all night on the wing. It flies at a height of 2–10 metres and often hovers near trees.
Body length: 4–5 cm

DATE_____

PLACE_____

PIPISTRELLE

Pipistrelles are Europe's smallest bats. They have short legs and tails, and narrow wings. The fur is dark and evenly coloured. Pipistrelles fly soon after sunset, occasionally even before sunset. They fly fast, with frequent twists and turns. Often roost in buildings in summer and hibernate in large colonies in winter.

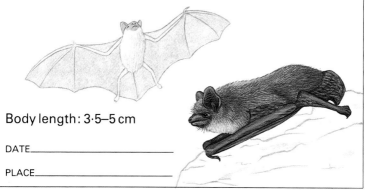

Body length: 3·5–5 cm

DATE_____

PLACE_____

43

Naturewatch Projects

Once you develop an interest in wildlife, there is no end to the things you can do. You might, for example, like to make a special study of a particular stretch of hedgerow near where you live, or perhaps your local park or a short stretch of a woodland stream. Your first interest might be to discover all the mammal life of the area, but all living things are linked together and very soon you will find yourself exploring the birdlife of the area as well, then the insect life and the plant life.

Every animal needs to eat, whether it is a browser or a grazer, a hunter or a scavenger. Try to find out who eats what. Some animals depend mainly on a single type of food while others eat a great variety of food. Food energy is passed from one animal to another along a 'food chain'. For example a cat might kill a shrew, which in turn may have eaten a beetle, which fed on caterpillars which lived on the young leaves of a nettle plant. Each stage in the chain is important. If one is destroyed, the whole chain is weakened. This is why naturalists seldom concentrate on only one group of animals. To understand any animal we have to understand the others in its food chain.

Life-styles and life-cycles

Another fascinating approach is to try to work out exactly how an animal spends its time throughout the year. Does it live alone for most of the time, or in a large group? Does the animal have a life-long mate or does it look for a new mate each year? What kind of nest or burrow does it make? When are the young born? Who feeds them, and who trains them to look after themselves as they grow?

If you study a particular animal you can build up a nature diary of the main events in its life. And if you enjoy taking photographs, or drawing, you can use these skills to illustrate the diary, or to make a wall display.

Observer's tricks

If you are lucky enough to find a place where small nocturnal animals have been feeding, you might want to return with an adult at night and try to catch a good view of them. If you do, take along a large flashlight or torch but tape some transparent red cellophane over the lens (a sweet wrapper will do). The soft red light will give you plenty of light to see by – and it won't frighten the animals.

Another useful tip is to put down some bait for the animal you want to watch. Then, if it does come along, at least it will stop for a while where you can see it easily, rather than trotting straight past you on its search for its evening meal. Try various combinations of cereals, oatmeal, chopped carrot and apple, nuts, raisins and ordinary birdseed. Make each mixture similar to the natural food of the animal you want to attract.

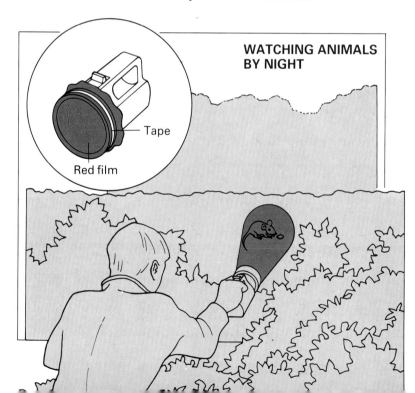

WATCHING ANIMALS BY NIGHT

Tape

Red film

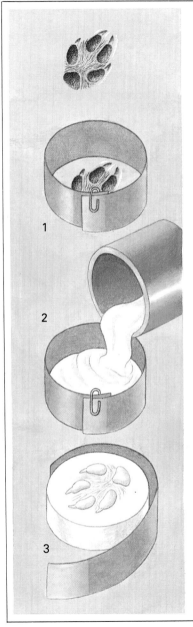

MAKING A PLASTER CAST

With a little care you can make perfect casts of animal footprints using plaster of Paris, available from most large chemists. (Pink wall plaster is not suitable.)

1. To hold the plaster, cut out a section from a plastic liquid container, or make a ring of stiff card. Press one of these into the earth around the track, carefully picking out any leaves or twigs that might spoil the cast.

2. Mix the plaster into a very smooth, soft, creamy paste. Pour it gently into the mould, using a spoon or stick to make sure it gets into every corner. Leave the plaster for at least 15 minutes before trying to lift it. (As it sets it gets warm at first, then cools quickly. Wait until it is quite cold.)

3. Finally, lift the mould and gently brush the loose dirt from the plaster. When you get home you can clean it up properly and, for effect, you can pick out the print using modelling paint.

Nature Clubs

Nature clubs and societies

One of the best ways of learning more about the wildlife of your area is to join a local naturalists' club. That way you will have a chance to go on short field trips and walks with people who have more experience. They will be able to point out tracks and signs you might otherwise miss, and they will be full of useful tips and hints about the best places to watch from, the best times, and so on.

Your local library will have the names and addresses of the various clubs in the area, and you might be surprised at just how many there are. As well as a ramblers' club, there will probably be a general naturalists' club, almost certainly at least one bird-watching society and perhaps other specialist clubs for people interested in mammals, insects or wild flowers. Your library will also have the addresses of the local branches of some of the larger national organizations.

Friends of the Zoo
The London Zoo, Regent's Park, London NW1 4RY

British Trust for Conservation Volunteers
36 St Mary's Street, Wallingford, Oxfordshire OX1 0EU

WATCH (Junior club of the Royal Society for Nature Conservation)
22 The Green, Nettleham, Lincoln LN2 2NR

The Mammal Society (Junior Branch)
141 Newmarket Road, Cambridge CB5 8HA

World Wildlife Fund
Panda House, 11–13 Ockford Road, Godalming, Surrey GU7 1QU

Young Ornithologists' Club
The Lodge, Sandy, Bedfordshire SG19 2DL

Index

Alpine marmot 29
Atlantic grey seal 39

Badger 10, 12, 16
Bank vole 24
Bats 20, 21, 36, 38, 41, 43
Black rat 42
Blue hare 28
Boar, wild 12, 17
Bottlenosed dolphin 40
Brown hare 31
Brown rat 42

Cat, wild 26, 28
Chamois 27
Common dolphin 40
Common dormouse 24
Common seal 38
Common shrew 33
Common long-eared bat
    43
Common vole 25
Conservation 3, 4, 47
Coypu 35

Daubenton's bat 36
Deer 9, 12, 13, 14, 26, 34, 41
Desman, Pyrenean 35
Dolphins 38, 40
Dormice 19, 24

Edible dormouse 19

Fallow deer 13
Field mouse 19, 41; yellow-
    necked 19
Fox 5, 8, 9, 10, 12, 17, 34

Grey squirrel 8, 12, 18
Ground vole 37

Hares 10, 26, 28, 31, 41
Harvest mouse 32
Hedgehog 22, 23, 38, 41
House mouse 41

Lesser horseshoe bat 20

Marmots 29
Mice 8, 19, 31, 32, 41
Mole 10, 32
Mouflon 27
Muntjac 14

Noctule bat 21

Otter 5, 10, 34

Pilot whale 39
Pine marten 12, 16
Pipistrelle 43
Polecat 15
Porpoise 38
Pygmy shrew 25

Rabbit 5, 7, 9, 30
Rats 41, 42
Red deer 9, 26
Red squirrel 12, 18
Roe deer 5, 13

Seals 38, 39
Sheep, wild 26, 27
Short-tailed vole 29
Shrews 22, 25, 33, 36, 44
Sika deer 14
Squirrels 5, 8, 10, 12, 18, 38
Stoat 5, 12, 15

Voles 10, 22, 24, 25, 26, 29, 37

Walrus 38
Water shrew 34, 36
Water vole 7, 34, 37
Weasel 8, 23
Whales 38, 39
Whiskered bat 21
White-toothed shrew 33
Wood mouse 10, 31, 41

Yellow-necked field mouse 19